TREASURES
OF
THE FRICK ART MUSEUM

TEXT BY
WALTER READ HOVEY

THE FRICK ART MUSEUM
PITTSBURGH, PENNSYLVANIA
1975

Published in 1975 by The Helen Clay Frick Foundation, Pittsburgh, Pennsyl-
vania, simultaneously in the United States and Canada. All rights reserved in
countries of the International Union for the Protection of Literary and Artistic
Works.
Library of Congress Cataloging in Publication Data: The Frick Art Museum,
Pittsburgh. Treasures of The Frick Art Museum. Includes index. 1. Art, Pitts-
burgh. 2. The Frick Art Museum, Pittsburgh. I. Hovey, Walter Read, 1895.
II. Title. N710.5.A87; 708'.14'886; 75–26681.
Printed and bound by Conzett + Huber AG, Zurich, Switzerland.

The Frick Art Museum was dedicated for
the enjoyment of the people of Pittsburgh in the
year nineteen hundred and seventy. This book illustrates
the works of art belonging to the Museum
five years later.

ACKNOWLEDGMENTS

Photography: HAROLD CORSINI, Pittsburgh, Pennsylvania
Grateful acknowledgment is made to all who have been helpful in the accomplishment of this publication.
Quotation on p. 9 from George Harvey, *Henry Clay Frick, The Man,*
Charles Scribner's Sons, New York, 1928.

TABLE OF CONTENTS

INTRODUCTION

Five years ago, in October of 1970, Miss Helen Clay Frick opened a museum of art in Pittsburgh, located in Point Breeze, across from the Homewood Avenue entrance to Frick Park. It has an interesting history. More than fifty years ago the distinguished collection of Henry Clay Frick had been given to the city of New York. He had hoped to keep it in Pittsburgh, and had actually engaged one of America's outstanding architects, Daniel Burnham, to draw up plans for a house with an adequate gallery which was to have been built on what was then called Clayton Heights, now Frick Park. But feeling that the smoke from the steel mills in nearby Homestead would eventually cause considerable damage to his paintings, regrettably, he took them to New York. In so doing, of course, he was making them available to many more people than would have seen them in Pittsburgh.

The story of the collection Mr. Frick assembled and opened to the public in a handsome setting which became his home, has been admirably told in *Masterpieces of The Frick Collection* by the late Harry D. M. Grier, formerly director of The Collection, and Edgar Munhall, curator. Mr. Frick had a rare instinctive awareness of quality which resulted in the uniqueness of the masterpieces he acquired as well as the exquisite taste of their arrangement in The Frick Collection. And he said: " . . . I can only hope that the public will get one half the

pleasure that has been afforded me in the enjoyment of these masterpieces in proper surroundings." Thus by example he was, in a very real sense, the inspiration for the museum his daughter has built in Pittsburgh. Responsibly, and with imagination she has assumed a heritage following her father in motive, perceptiveness, and taste.

In her enthusiasm for Pittsburgh, and enlarging this interest, Miss Frick established in 1927 a department of art history at the University of Pittsburgh. Special emphasis was placed on the assembling of an outstanding fine arts library begun by Frederick Mortimer Clapp and developed by Walter Read Hovey into one of the finest of its kind in the country. Further expansion took place in the early 1960's with the construction of a special art building designed in the Renaissance style and called The Henry Clay Frick Fine Arts Building, in memory of her father. It was intended to be a center of first importance dedicated to historical, critical, and technical studies of the arts with some emphasis upon training in conservation. Most importantly it was to include the gradual acquisition of an outstanding and representative collection. The building contains the library, class rooms, laboratories, a handsome auditorium, and galleries.

Of singular significance, as part of the total plan, was the open court and glassed-in walks in the center of the building recalling the charming cloistered areas of the Florentine Renaissance. It was dedicated to Dr. John G. Bowman who brought distinction to the University as its chancellor, and whose enthusiasm and interest were of great encouragement to Miss Frick in her admirable objectives. She planned this court for the express purpose of installing twenty-two unique reconstructions of some of the best known frescoes of the Renaissance which were gradually deteriorating and likely to perish before too long through increasingly damaging atmospheric conditions in Europe.

These have an interesting history. They had been painted early in the twentieth century by a talented Russian artist, Nicholas Lochoff, for the Moscow Museum of Fine Arts after considerable scholarly research in the various methods of the old masters in fresco, tempera, and oil. However, most of the collection remained in Lochoff's studio in Florence because the Revolution in Russia prevented the Tsar from ultimately acquiring it. Eventually a number of examples became available for purchase. Several were bought for American museums such as the Fogg Art Museum at Harvard University. Miss Frick acquired most of them for her plan for the art development at the University of Pittsburgh. In the opinion of Bernard Berenson these had great importance for the student both from the point of view of the technique and connoisseurship. Thus the court of the new building enriched with these outstanding frescoes afforded an unusual opportunity for students and public alike.

Miss Frick's further plan, however, did not fit into the thinking of an interim administration at the University. She decided that her original wish for Pittsburgh, and that of her father before her, could best be satisfied by the building of an independent art museum. Her enthusiasm for the new museum prompted her almost immediately to enlarge the collection already begun for the University and to make it available as soon as possible, thus bringing to fruition a concept of many years before. Miss Frick's wish was to create in her museum here the same delightfully warm and intimate atmosphere which one senses so keenly in walking through The Frick Collection in New York. The presence of fresh flowers in the galleries adds greatly to the enjoyment of the visitor and the museum collection, a very personal one, has been held to the highest standards of quality.

The building itself appropriately reflects the spirit of the Renaissance and the architects, Pratt, Schafer, and Slowik, of Pittsburgh, have shown a sensitive understanding of the principles of scale and proportion that were practised in the fifteenth century by such great architects as the Florentine Brunellesco. It was built by all local craftsmen of Alabama limestone, suggesting in its color and veining the quality of marble and contrasting effectively with the green-glazed terra cotta tile roof. The red and pink marbles used in the interior were quarried in northern Italy near Lake Garda and in the Sierra de Sintra region of Portugal. Aside from their intrinsic beauty they offer intriguing entertainment in the discovery of various fossil forms incorporated in the natural pattern of the stone. The interior of the building is for the most part Burmese and African teak, American walnut, and Honduras mahogany. Samples of all the materials with labels stating where they are

from and where they are used have been mounted and hang in the North Corridor of the Museum.

Concerts are held in the auditorium approximately once a month. The Museum has its own handsome harpsichord which is a copy of a French instrument of 1770 by Pascal Taskin in the Louis XVI style. The Museum also owns a set of Musical Glasses, or Grand Harmonicon, an instrument which was popular in fashionable circles in the eighteenth century. It dates from about 1825 and was a gift from a dear friend of the Frick family, Mrs. McCook Knox of Washington, D.C. The concerts, like those in The Frick Collection in New York, are open to the public without charge, but admission is by ticket.

One cannot measure the far-reaching significance of this generous gift for the benefit of all the people. In ideal surroundings works of art and music may be enjoyed with the pleasure of a very personal contact.

Virginia E. Lewis
Director
The Frick Art Museum

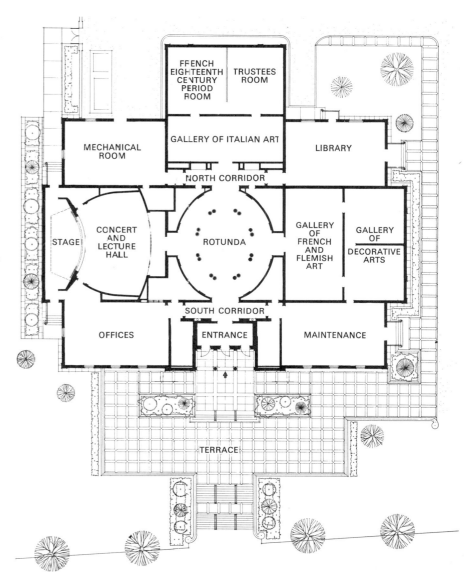

ROTUNDA

VIEW FROM SOUTH

On entering the building of The Frick Art Museum the visitor finds himself surrounded by the handsome oval foyer often adorned with flowering plants which, with the slightly curved and luminous ceiling, suggests an open court and makes a transition from the outside world to the more rarefied atmosphere within. Here the spirit or general tone of the Collection is announced, for the tapestry hangings, although from regions north of the Alps, belong to the period of transition from the Middle Ages to the Renaissance, and the great urn in the center, actually from the terrace at Versailles, represents the taste at the end of the eighteenth century. The perspective terminates with a view into the gallery of Italian paintings while on the cross axis one sees on the right the gallery of French and Flemish works, on the left, the handsome auditorium.

The rapid growth of interest in the arts today has resulted in many new museum buildings, some emphasizing a contemporary style, others more academic traditions and adherence to the classical forms of the past. Very few make any effort to relate the architecture to the collections within. Of course, with large city museums where collections cover many centuries this is impossible. But here, where the ideal of art corresponds to the flow of ideas in Europe from the

CLAUDE MICHEL, CALLED CLODION,
FRENCH, 1738–1814
Carved Marble Urn:
Classical Scene with Satyr
Height: 53 in. (134.6 cm.)

earliest beginnings of the Renaissance through the eighteenth century, a building showing a respect for that style, which began in Florence during the fifteenth century and continued in France with such buildings as the Petit Trianon in the eighteenth century, not only pays tribute to that great cultural tradition but enhances the collections within.

The spacious interior of the Rotunda and well-proportioned teakwood columns make an ideal setting for a large marble urn (p. 14) by the eighteenth-century French sculptor, Claude Michel, known as Clodion. This is one of a set made for the terrace at Versailles, two of which are now in the National Gallery in Washington. As a foremost exponent of the rococo spirit, we see here in this work of Clodion that combination of architectural principles with the animation and briskness of movement characteristic of the period which was soon to result in the less imaginative phase of the Classical Revival. On the one side the sculptor has carved a satyr who with the help of a young couple is trying to erect a herm, thus coyly suggesting an erotic idea. On the other side (p. 15) is a similar scene of a young woman and child as satyrs. These figures are very like those on the lunette by Clodion from the *Hôtel de Condé* done in the same year. The perfect classical shape of the urn has been adorned with a garland of grapes, ribbons, and

CLAUDE MICHEL, CALLED CLODION
Carved Marble Urn – Detail:
Satyress and Child Satyr

15

large ram's head handles in the spirit of the eighteenth century. It has been signed and dated C. M. Clodion./F. 1782.

The walls are hung with tapestries, adding color and richness of texture. Of special interest are two large fragments in the millefleurs tradition, the one representing the theme of the Concert (p. 16), the other (p. 17), an elegant lady with two smaller figures as attendants. They were woven in the valley of the Loire about 1500, impressive reminders of the Age of Chivalry just then coming to a close. Indeed they suggest the famous Unicorn tapestries at the Cluny Museum in Paris or those in the Cloisters in New York. One of the great decorative accomplishments in art, they have a deeper significance through the theme of music where a man plays the flute, a lady, the dulcimer, and again in the field of flowers, executed almost as botanical studies, so accurately are they rendered. The catalogue of a recent exhibition held at the Metropolitan Museum of Art in New York, *Masterpieces of Tapestry from the Fourteenth to the Sixteenth Century* written by Geneviève Souchal, refers to the rarity of the Concert theme and the fact that the principal figures here are identical to those of a tapestry in the Cluny Museum. Of course the mediaeval theme of the closed garden brought a rich symbolism of flowers into art, but here

FRENCH, SCHOOL OF THE LOIRE,
CA. 1500
Millefleurs Tapestry:
Lady and Attendant
94 × 68 in. (241.2 × 172.6 cm.)

FLEMISH, EARLY XVI CENTURY
Tapestry: Court of Love
107 × 136 in. (271.8 × 345.2 cm.)

as decoration for a great feudal chateau their use was probably the result of a growing interest in the beauty of the physical world.

The use of allegory became extremely popular in the court art of this period, and there is an exquisite example of this, *Court of Love* (p. 18), a Brussels weave of the early sixteenth century. Here the court is held out-of-doors amidst a fanfare of trumpets. The fountain of life suggests Nature's abundance so beautifully expressed in the border while the crescent moon above the horizon reminds one of her mystery. It is undoubtedly a scene derived from the *Minnekönigen* and was formerly in the von Pannwitz collection.

A return to the more specifically religious subjects and smaller weaves occurred in the sixteenth century. We see this in another product of the Brussels looms representing the *Rest on the Flight into Egypt*. This example (p. 19) is thought to have formerly decorated the private chapel at Knole House in Kent, and must have been woven in the first third of the sixteenth century. It is interesting to see how the convention of a decorative border persists, now like a frame embracing a panoramic view of the world. The seemingly infinite space and attention to detail suggests a derivation from paintings such as those of Joachim Patenier while one recalls a fifteenth-century print of Martin Schongauer with angels hidden in the foliage of the tree against which the Madonna rests. Her rich robe contains gold threads in contrast to the plain wool of the weaving of the lowly donkey behind her. Many apocryphal legends developed in regard to the Flight into Egypt. Perhaps this delight in a beautiful landscape with infinite space goes back to the teachings of Cusanus, Bishop of Brixen, in the preceding century, for he believed in the apprehension of God through the beauty of Nature.

FLEMISH, EARLY XVI CENTURY

Tapestry: Rest on the Flight
into Egypt

92 × 85 in. (233.6 × 215.8 cm.)

NORTH CORRIDOR

VIEW LOOKING INTO GALLERY OF
ITALIAN ART

I n passing from the Rotunda to the Gallery of Italian Art directly opposite the entrance one crosses a corridor where Chinese porcelains purchased by Mr. Frick from the Morgan collection are displayed. The discovery of Chinese art, made manifest largely through the importation of their ceramics, had great importance in the development of the decorative arts of France during the eighteenth century. As a collector Mr. Frick early sensed the beauty of the asymmetrical and colorful enamel patterns on the vases and their appropriateness as accents in an eighteenth-century interior. Examples in the collection of The Frick Art Museum are from the late seventeenth on through the eighteenth century and represent the famous underglaze blue from the time of K'ang Hsi to the brilliant enamels of Ch'ien Lung.

The use of blue in Chinese ceramics is fascinating, both as an indication of contacts with Persia through the centuries and the superiority of Chinese technical achievements. Cobalt from which the color was derived was brought from Persia at great expense and, therefore, was not much used until the establishment of the Imperial kilns. A pair of large vases in the Museum dating from the reign of K'ang Hsi (1662–1722) are beautifully painted in underglaze blue. There is also a pair of powder blue vases in the Collection which were made at the royal kilns of Ching-te-Chên early in the eighteenth century. These kilns were especially supported by the Emperor

CHINESE PORCELAIN,
REIGN OF CH'IEN LUNG, 1736–1795
Punch bowls with lotus motif
Height: 6½ in. (16.5 cm.)
Diameter: 15⅜ in. (39.1 cm.)

K'ang Hsi. His long reign is often compared to that of his contemporary, Louis XIV of France. As the founder of the Ching dynasty he was eager to maintain the Chinese cultural tradition which had been sponsored by the preceding Ming rulers. This development of an even-blue ground was accomplished by a new spraying process.

Especially fine is a pair of large, bottle-shaped vases typical of the Ch'ien Lung period with *famille rose* enamels, one showing the peach, the other, the chrysanthemum (p. 23). As a pair they may have represented the seasons of spring and fall. Almost every object used in Chinese art has a symbolic significance and was repeated again and again. Because of the long life of its stone, the peach is often used as a symbol of longevity.

CHINESE PORCELAIN,
REIGN OF CH'IEN LUNG, 1736–1795
Pair of bottle-shape vases,
famille rose, enamel colors
Height: 20 in. (50.8 cm.)
Circumference: 46½ in. (118.1 cm.)

CHINESE PORCELAIN, REIGN OF K'ANG HSI, 1662–1722
Vases, famille verte, enamel colors
Height: 18⅛ in. (46 cm.); 18³/₁₆ in. (46.2 cm.)

MEISSEN PORCELAIN, CA. 1735
Pair of vases
Height: 19½ in. (49.5 cm.)

The cases in the corridor to the right contain excellent examples of the famous *famille rose* and *famille verte* enamel decorations, and also date from the eighteenth century (p. 24). As often happens in the arts the over-elaboration of enamel decoration tended to lose the ceramic refinement and ultimately a decadence set in.

Of considerable historic value is a pair of Meissen vases made in the Chinese style (p. 25). Stylistically they must date about 1735 and they have the Meissen mark of crossed swords in underglaze blue on the bottom. It must be admitted that the shape lacks the crisp refinement of the best Chinese pieces, and the drawing in the reserves does not have their precision of style. The secret of hard-paste porcelain, known to the Chinese for many years, had only been achieved in the

FLEMISH, XVII CENTURY
Bronze Figure of a Dog
Height: 7⅝ in. (19.4 cm.)

West about 1710 by Boettger who was probably more interested in alchemy than in aesthetics. These vases with white reserves on a magenta ground might well have been copies from Chinese examples of the period and are important documents of the relation between Europe and China at this early period.

Also between the Rotunda and the Gallery of Italian Art, and as in The Frick Collection in New York, scattered throughout the Museum, there are a few small Renaissance bronzes. Shown here (p. 26, 27) are two examples—a dog and a bull—which were probably part of a hunt group comprised of many figures. These were considered by Wilhelm von Bode to be seventeenth-century Flemish, but more recent scholarship has suggested a Venetian origin.

FLEMISH, XVII CENTURY
Bronze Figure of a Bull
Height: 7 in. (17.8 cm.)

GALLERY OF ITALIAN ART

VIEW OF EAST END OF GALLERY

The Gallery of Italian Art with its beamed ceiling and dado paneling, terra cotta tiled floor, red damask wall covering, and fifteenth-century Florentine stone fireplace provides an appropriate setting for its paintings. The range of interest here extends from the thirteenth into the seventeenth century, but the overshadowing love for the Italian primitive is apparent. It is interesting to consider these early works both as final expressions of the Age of Faith, at least in Italy, and as steps leading into the Renaissance. To Italy, the innovator of the tradition of panel painting for the western world, belongs the great achievement of the new spirit of humanism.

Although great emphasis has been placed on the classical background in Italy as bringing this about, the teachings of Saint Francis had far-reaching effects. It was through them that individual emotions, so characteristic of the Renaissance, came to be realized. But the mediaeval spirit called for an hieratic, impersonal expression which had its source largely in the more formalized

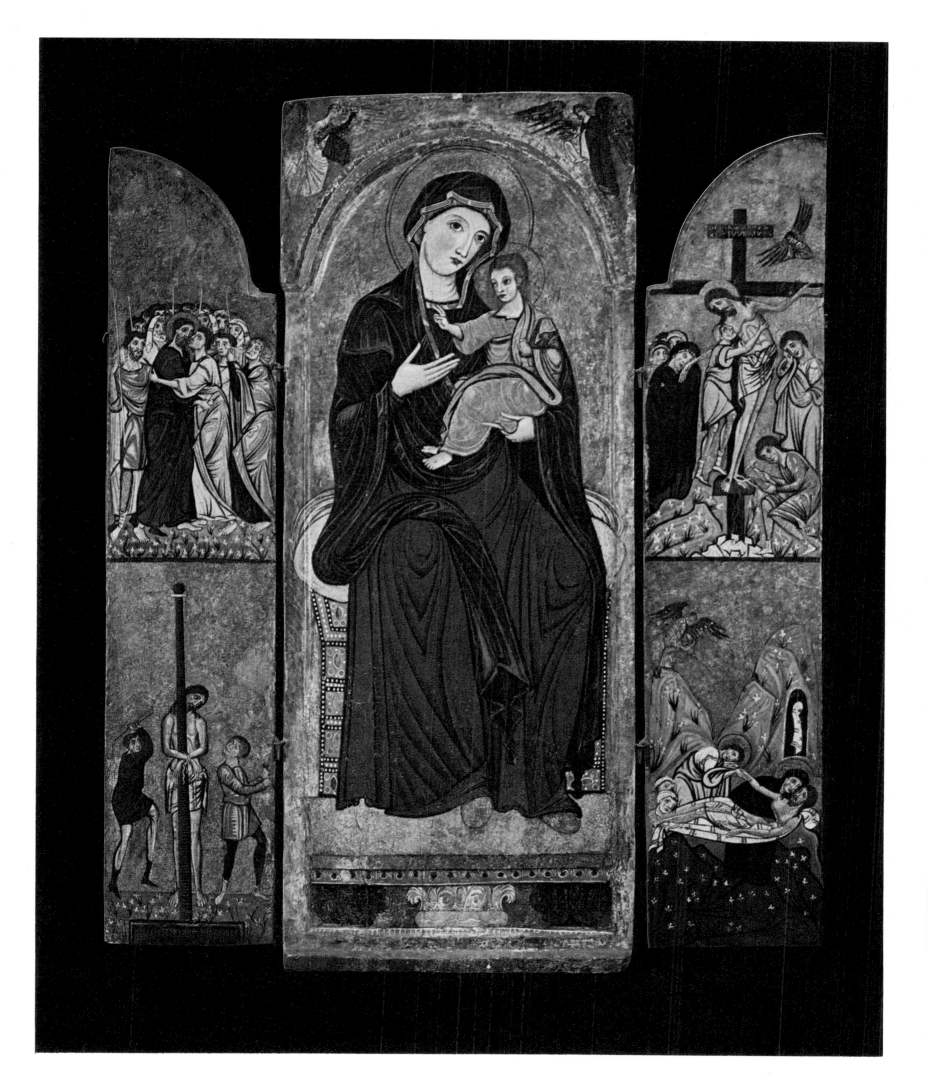

SCHOOL OF LUCCA TRIPTYCH, CLOSED:
Saint Francis and Saint Anthony
49¾ × 20 in. (126.3 × 50.8 cm.)

FOLLOWER OF GIOTTO,
ROMAGNOLE SCHOOL, CA. 1266–1337
Madonna and Child with Saints,
Scenes from the Life
of Christ and the Virgin
Triptych: tempera, on panels
28¾ × 38¾ in. (73 × 98.4 cm.)

FOLLOWER OF GIOTTO, ▷
ROMAGNOLE SCHOOL
Madonna and Child with Saints,
Scenes from the Life of Christ
and the Virgin – Detail:
Christ Mounting the Cross
7³/₁₆ × 5 in. (18.2 × 12.7 cm.)

DUCCIO DI BUONINSEGNA, SIENESE, ▷▷
CA. 1278–1319
Angel with Crown of Thorns and
Spear
Tempera, on panel
9¾ × 6½ in. (24.8 × 16.5 cm.)

art of the Near East. These stylizations were not easily overcome. To Siena belongs the credit of enlivening the old established forms while Florence developed a new style based more on an awareness of the physical world.

Panel paintings from the thirteenth century are extremely rare. An important example is a triptych, *Madonna and Child Enthroned with Four Scenes of the Passion* (p. 31), probably a traveling altar, from a Franciscan priory in the region of Lucca, and which must date around 1270. On the doors, observable when closed, are representations of Saint Francis and Saint Anthony (p. 32). One senses the Byzantine background in the stylized drapery folds, the rich ornamentation of

SIENESE, XIV CENTURY
Madonna and Child with
Saint Catherine and Saint John
Tempera, on panel
15¼ × 7⅛ in. (38.7 × 18.1 cm.)

BERNARDO DADDI, FLORENTINE, ▷
CA. 1290–CA. 1348
Madonna and Child with Saint
Francis and a Bishop; Saint Peter
and Saint Paul; Crucifixion;
Annunciation
Triptych: tempera, on panels
17¼ × 16¾ in. (43.8 × 42.6 cm.)

FRANCESCO DI VANNUCCIO,
SIENESE, ACT. 1361–1388
Saint Catherine of Alexandria
Tempera, on panel
21½ × 14⅝ in. (54.6 × 37.2 cm.)

LIPPO MEMMI, SIENESE, 1285–1361 ▷
Saint Agnes; Saint Anthony
Tempera, on two panels
16¼ × 15 in. (41 × 38 cm.)

38

MATTEO DI GIOVANNI, SIENESE,
CA. 1430–1495
Madonna and Child with Saint
Jerome, Saint Sebastian and Angels
Tempera, on panel
29½ × 19¼ in. (74.9 × 48.9 cm.)

40

ARCANGELO DI COLA DA CAMERINO,
CA. 1385–1450
Madonna and Child Enthroned;
Crucifixion
Diptych: tempera, on panels
12 × 13¾ in. (30.5 × 35 cm.)

the throne and the composition of the four scenes of the Passion, yet the creativity of a great new tradition, which here seems purely mediaeval and of the West, is announced. The Madonna scarcely represents the Queen of Heaven as she leans, almost tenderly, towards the Christ Child and some feeling of individual human emotion pervades the other figures as well. The silver leaf ground is most unusual as is the representation of a Corinthian capital beneath the throne of the Madonna. Italian art came to stand for the dignity of the individual and his varied emotions.

Duccio of Siena is usually credited as the key figure in the establishment of the Sienese tradition, while Giotto of Florence, only slightly younger, is famed as the innovator of a style which was to blossom into the Renaissance. The gallery contains on the east wall a small but majestic figure of an archangel holding a crown of thorns and a spear, undoubtedly from the workshop of Duccio, and probably a pinnacle from his famous altarpiece painted for the Cathedral of

41

MASTER OF THE BAMBINO VISPO
Madonna and Child with
Scroll – Detail: Madonna

MASTER OF THE BAMBINO VISPO, ▷
FLORENTINE, ACT. 1400–1425
Madonna and Child with Scroll
Oil, and tempera, on panel
33 ¼ × 23 ⅜ in. (84.4 × 59.4 cm.)

STEFANO DI GIOVANNI,
CALLED SASSETTA
Madonna and Child with
Two Angels – Detail:
Madonna and Child

STEFANO DI GIOVANNI, ▷
CALLED SASSETTA, SIENESE,
1391/1400–1450
Madonna and Child with
Two Angels
Tempera, on panel
14½ × 10⅜ in. (36.8 × 26.3 cm.)

44

45

STEFANO DI GIOVANNI,
CALLED SASSETTA, SIENESE,
1391/1400–1450
Annunciation – Detail: The Virgin

Siena (p. 35). Certainly it is a masterpiece possessing the monumentality and individuality characteristic of Duccio. Both the subject, Saint Michael, and the shape of the panel attest the connection with the famous Sienese altarpiece.

In comparing the Museum triptych assigned to the School of Giotto, *Madonna and Child with
Saints, Scenes from the Life of Christ and the Virgin* (p. 33), with the earlier one just mentioned
from Lucca, one is struck by how firmly established were the old conventions. However, the
change of mood from dogma to individual participation begins to be apparent. Now as a museum
piece these panels have been firmly placed in a modern frame decorated with geometrical motifs
of the period. Bernard Berenson has suggested that they may have been executed by a follower
of Giotto who worked with him on the frescoes in the Arena Chapel at Padua. The Giottesque
characteristics are noticeable in the rendering of the draperies which lack the Byzantine linear
stylizations, and shadows here and there make an attempt to express form.

An unusual scene and one indicating a change of spirit, in the small panels of the Giottesque
triptych illustrating the lives of Christ and the Virgin, is the one where Christ mounts the ladder
leaning against the Cross as though cooperating with his executioners (p. 34). It derives from the
Meditationes of Saint Bonaventura who, writing in the thirteenth century, described in detail the
emotions and sufferings of Christ. Yet these small panels maintain the old Byzantine conventions,

46

such as the Nativity taking place in a cave or the Dormition of the Virgin and the Descent into Hell, scenes that show the symbolism of the Eastern church as distinct from that of the West. Perhaps an illuminating comparison is to be found in the scene of the Betrayal in the two paintings.

Towards the middle of the fourteenth century there was such a demand for small altar paintings that the artists, following the custom in other trades, became organized into corporations, and Bernardo Daddi was the administrator of one of these groups. He was extremely popular. The scalloped drapery of the throne as shown in the example of his work in the Museum (p. 37) is characteristic. Painted about 1335 this triptych, as is often the case with works of this period, has been put into a modern frame. Some Sienese influences are evident although it belongs to the Florentine school. The Christ Child begins to show animation and Mary kneeling at the foot of the Cross intensifies the emotion. Daddi died of the plague, the Black Death, in 1348.

The little panel of the Madonna and Child holding a bird (p. 36) also shows both Florentine and Sienese influences. But the interest of the artist, however slight, tends to be in the development of form rather than in the more decorative line so characteristic of the Sienese. The figure on the left is Saint John, patron saint of Florence. On the right is Saint Catherine of Alexandria rather than Catherine of Siena for she is crowned and wears the regal ermine. The symbol of the goldfinch when held by the Christ Child portends the Crown of Thorns.

GIOVANNI DI PAOLO
Nativity – Detail:
Annunciation to the Shepherds

Religious fervor as the result of the decimation of the population at this time through the plague greatly increased the demand for small altars and emphasized a pessimistic note in the painting. Then the popularity of the Italian primitive early in this century meant that many altars which had been neglected were broken up and sold. The two panels portraying Saint Agnes and Saint Anthony (p. 39) were obviously part of a larger work. Berenson has attributed them to Lippo Memmi on stylistic grounds, but Professor Federico Zeri of the University of Rome has made a stronger case for Lippo Vanni. He refers to an altar which had been broken up, one section of which is now in the Metropolitan Museum in New York, another in the Rhode Island School of Design in Providence, Rhode Island, as having close stylistic resemblances.

Another painting of the period showing strong Sienese characteristics, even the idealized monumentality of Duccio's archangel, is the Saint Catherine of Alexandria by Francesco di Vannuccio (p. 38). Although there is almost no scholarly documentation about her, she ranks as one of the fourteen most helpful saints in Heaven. Possibly the fact that she was a queen gave her special prominence. Here her beauty, golden hair and regal garb, form a strange contrast to her sad expression and her symbols of martyrdom. Never was mystical figure more forceful. She somehow bears in her expression the sufferings of humanity. She is the epitome of the dramatic power of Sienese art before it became softened by pictorial charm. This is said to be Vannuccio's masterpiece.

GIOVANNI DI PAOLO, SIENESE, ▷
CA. 1403–1482
Nativity
Tempera, on panel
23 × 17¼ in. (58.4 × 43.8 cm.)

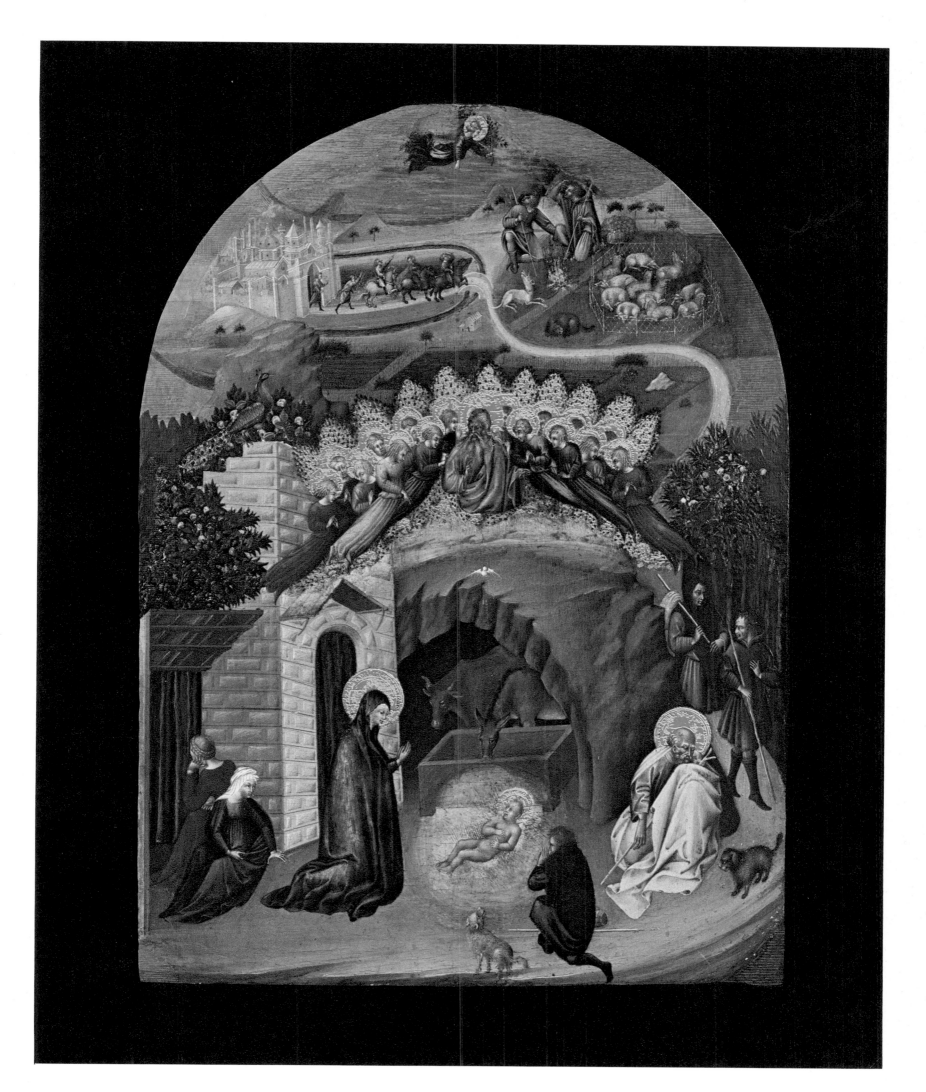

In Arcangelo di Cola da Camerino we see an artist content with the taste of his surroundings but who has unconsciously absorbed a few elements of a new approach. The Museum diptych by him, *Madonna and Child Enthroned, Crucifixion* (p. 41), must have been executed about 1425, yet it follows the fourteenth-century tradition. It shows an awareness of what Florentine painting was beginning to achieve, that is, spatial feeling and the representation of the physical world. In the Madonna panel the angels are definitely behind the throne. They peek through its openings and the throne itself is drawn in perspective. Obviously Arcangelo was familiar with Giotto's majestic retable in the church of the Ognissanti in Florence but he adds a little more form, a sculpturesque quality to his figures. This is especially obvious in the modeling of the body of Christ on the Cross and the light on the figures below.

On the back of the Crucifixion panel "D Camerino Arcangelus Pinsit" is written. This might have been copied from an inscription which was destroyed when the panels were separated, as we know they were, when in the collection of Mrs. Longland at Abingdon near Oxford. At any rate this gives a clue as to the artist, and in comparison with details in rendering in other

APOLLONIO DI GIOVANNI
Scenes from The Odyssey:
Story of Penelope – Detail:
Penelope at Her Loom

53

that virtue, even though she has a radiant halo in gold and sumptuously garbed angels hold a jeweled crown above her head. She is the Queen of Heaven but possesses the humble sentiment of a human mother. This painting has been compared to a similar panel in Berlin.

It is from the Berlin example, parts of which have been dispersed, that Professor Zeri feels certain that the two small panels of the Annunciation (p. 47) in the Museum collection came. These works by Sassetta are expressions of a phase of European thought of the early fifteenth century which became popular through the great work *The Imitation of Christ* by Thomas à Kempis.

This rare and simple mysticism soon became overshadowed in art by the famous International style which had spread from Avignon, where the popes resided during the fourteenth century. It brought decorative and pictorial attributes, the charm of court and aristocratic patronage into religious art. The works of Giovanni di Paolo (1403–1483), a contemporary and friend of Sassetta, beautifully embody this influence. In his painting of the Nativity, about 1450, he has included in a charming overall composition the concept of the Trinity, The Adoration of the Virgin, the Adoration of the Shepherds, the Annunciation to them, their journey and the Journey of the Wise Men (p. 49). The great distance which they must travel is naively indicated by a curved route leading from an oriental city having a domed building, suggesting in miniature the Cathedral of Florence. All is done in a style similar to that found in illuminated manuscripts such as the *Très Riches Heures* of the Duc de Berry of a slightly earlier period.

The last great exponent of Sienese art in the fifteenth century was Matteo di Giovanni (ca. 1430–1495), represented in the Museum by a late work similar to one in the Metropolitan

APOLLONIO DI GIOVANNI,
FLORENTINE, CA. 1415–1465
Scenes from The Odyssey:
Story of Penelope

Tempera, on cassone panel
7½ × 37⅜ in. (19 × 94.9 cm.)

works has isolated a group. Certainly the Madonna is similar to one in the gallery at Camerino.

Siena, however, is the city in Italy where the tender delicacy of mediaeval emotion persisted longest, only slightly touched by the new spirit of the Renaissance. This phase of expression is exquisitely rendered in the gallery by two works of Sassetta and one by his younger contemporary, Giovanni di Paolo. It is announced in the painting *Madonna and Child with Scroll* (p. 43), by the Master of the Bambino Vispo (restless child). Here we see a youthful Madonna plainly clothed against an elaborately tooled gold background and seated on a bolster which rests on material of the richest design and color, a strange contrast of wealth and humility. Even the frame is adorned with three painted medallions, God rushing through space to create the world, and the Angel and the Virgin of the Annunciation. The decorative use of fabrics indicates a return to prosperity and is characteristic of the International style which developed at the Papal court of Avignon in the fourteenth century. In our painting the all-too-robust Christ Child holds a scroll saying *Ego sum via.* Other works have been isolated as being by this artist and the name Parri Spinelli has been suggested. In any event it must date from the early years of the fifteenth century and is probably not even by a Sienese artist.

Sassetta, whose real name was Stefano di Giovanni (1391–1450), represents the ultimate refinement of sensibilities in the Sienese tradition as in the painting *Madonna and Child with Two Angels* (p. 45), dating from about 1424. Still working in the spirit of the Middle Ages like his contemporary Fra Angelico, he was aware of the new conventions regarding form and space but somehow felt them irrelevant to his theme. Rarely has the style of a work so beautifully reflected the pure, uncluttered spirit of a religious ideal. His Madonna of Humility in this painting still bespeaks

FRANCESCO UBERTINI,
CALLED IL BACCHIACCA
Madonna and Child with Saint
Elizabeth and Saint John – Detail:
The Beggars

FRANCESCO UBERTINI,
CALLED IL BACCHIACCA, FLORENTINE,
CA. 1494–1557
Madonna and Child with
Saint Elizabeth and Saint John
Oil, on panel
47¾ × 35⅝ in. (121.3 × 90.5 cm.)

FRANCESCO MELZI, MILANESE,
1493–CA. 1570
Madonna and Child in a
Jasmine Bower
Oil, on panel
34⅜ × 26 in. (87.3 × 66 cm.)

Museum in New York (p. 40). It was probably done for a private patron, and the more careful modeling indicates the growing domination of Florentine taste. Saint Jerome and Saint Sebastian are on either side of the Virgin and Child with two angels above. It was, of course, this new technical interest in realistic representation, combined with a more sophisticated patronage and interest in the Classical tradition, which ultimately made Florence the center of the early Renaissance.

The great achievement of Florence in the fifteenth century was the fusion of classical philosophical concepts with mediaeval theology. Occasionally subjects taken directly from classical literature were used with religious overtones, and secular painting became more and more popular as commercial activity increased. Marriage chests were popular furnishings for a patrician family and were often painted by artists of considerable talent. The transition into the scientific and psychological interests of the modern world now quickly took place.

Apollonio di Giovanni, sometimes called the Vergil or Dido Master (1425–1465), headed a workshop which specialized in painted *cassoni* or wedding chests. His work, including The Frick

JACOPO ROBUSTI,
CALLED IL TINTORETTO,
VENETIAN, 1518–1594
Susannah and the Elders
Oil, on canvas
30 × 36⅝ in. (76.2 × 93 cm.)

Art Museum painting, *Scenes from the Odyssey: Story of Penelope* (p. 51), now framed and hanging at the left of the fireplace, has been recently published by Ellen Callmann in the Oxford Studies of Art and Architecture. She explains that about twenty-five centimeters at the left of this example have been cut off and that this fragment is now in the Fogg Art Museum at Harvard; also that it was painted in two registers, the lower one now much damaged and covered by the frame. She refers, however, to the exceptional quality of the figures shown and to its undoubted attribution. As seen now, Calypso stands at the extreme left, then Nausikaa and her maiden are shown taking Odysseus to Alkinous' palace in a chariot, and one sees the feast with Alkinous. This scene is terminated by some masts of sailboats, and immediately one comes on two suitors outside Penelope's room where she sits with her loom and finally Odysseus' head appears as he climbs the stairs into the room where Penelope sits.

Apollonio was above all a story teller and, although his scenes suggest illuminated manuscripts, it is unlikely that his work was so inspired. His compositions are individual and reveal an awareness of the most advanced movements of his time. Classical history must have had a great appeal for

him and always in his subjects one finds an appropriate relationship to their use. Certainly he greatly enriched the thought of the fifteenth century.

With the *Madonna and Child in a Jasmine Bower* (p. 55) by Francesco Melzi, who was working in the sixteenth century, all suggestion of the mediaeval style has been forgotten. The Child is an idealized babe, and the mother wears that all-knowing, yet enigmatic smile made famous by Leonardo da Vinci in his *Mona Lisa*. Air, laden with the scent of jasmine blossoms, circulates about the figures which are as though posed for only a moment. It is a psychological study rather than a formal statement of a religious doctrine. As is well known, Melzi was a young friend and pupil of Leonardo da Vinci to whom this painting when sold in the mid-nineteenth century was attributed.

The Madonna and Child with Saint Elizabeth and Saint John (p. 55) by Bacchiacca also shows an influence from Leonardo. This is noticeable in the head of the Virgin which is obviously derived from the head of Anne in his *Virgin and Child with Saint Anne,* now in the Louvre. It has been pointed out, and the painting illustrated, in the catalogue of an exhibition called *Bacchiacca*

ITALIAN, XVI CENTURY
Wrought Iron and Bronze
Bishop's Chair
Height: 34¼ in. (87 cm.)
Width: 27¼ in. (59.2 cm.)
Depth: 19½ in. (49.5 cm.)

and His Friends which was held at the Baltimore Museum of Art in 1961. Francesco Ubertini, called Il Bacchiacca (1494–1557), borrowed details from works of artists he admired, not as inspiration for his own creativity or as plagiarism, but more in flattery to those masters as justifiable adaptations. As an eclectic artist he was a forerunner of the Mannerist movement. The small background figures are to be found in an engraving, *The Beggars,* by Lucas van Leyden, and the trees have a marked similarity also to those of that artist. Prints by Northern artists were beginning to have importance in the Italian tradition of painting.

The Collection has one Venetian painting of the sixteenth century (p. 56). It is by Jacopo Robusti, called Il Tintoretto (1518–1594). The subject is *Susannah and the Elders* which may have some significance as an allegory in which the Church was being falsely accused by the Jews. Tintoretto has been referred to as the artist who led the way to the Baroque style. He was able to dramatize his subjects by creating a feeling on the part of the spectator of participation in the theme. There is no longer a background against which figures are posed but rather diagonal compositions or, as in our painting, a whirling movement which, together with lights and darks, creates a sense of change. Venice with its extraordinary effects of light had become the center of art. There is some thought that this painting may have been executed by Marietta, Tintoretto's favorite daughter, who often worked with him and skillfully adapted his style. However, it

PADUAN, MID–XVI CENTURY
Bronze Equestrian Figure
Height: 11¾ in. (29.9 cm.)

FERDINANDO TACCA, FLORENTINE, ▷
LATE XVI CENTURY
Bronze Figure of Diana the Huntress
Height: 15¾ in. (39.4 cm.)

incorporates certainly the essential characteristics of Tintoretto's personal style, and it is marked by the spirit of Venice at the height of her power when the luxury of the Near Eastern potentates gave a new glamour to Western traditions of science and religion. Professor Federico Zeri has stated that it is a very fine Tintoretto.

This theatrical tendency dominated the taste of the seventeenth century. The dramatic contrasts of light and dark by which it is accomplished is evident in *The Calling of Saint Peter and Saint Andrew* (p. 57) by Luca Giordano (1632–1705). This masterpiece of Baroque painting was executed in Naples where the fervor of Spanish influence emphasized the continuation of the religious subject in the patronage of the Court and the Church. Giordano did this same subject as a fresco in the church of San Martino, now a museum, in Naples.

The Italian and more intimate spirit of this gallery has been enhanced by a few pieces of sixteenth and seventeenth century furniture and some small Renaissance bronzes. One of the bronzes, on the refectory table in the center, represents Diana as the huntress (p. 59). This was once considered to be Flemish but has now been suggested by Anthony Radcliffe to be by the Florentine sculptor, Ferdinando Tacca, active in the sixteenth century. Another bronze figure, of a rider on a rearing horse (p. 59), similar to one in the Rijksmuseum in Amsterdam, is in the style of Tiziano Aspetti who worked extensively in Venice during the late sixteenth century.

TRUSTEES ROOM

VIEW TOWARD NORTHEAST

JOHN HOPPNER, ENGLISH, 1758–1810
Princess Sophia, daughter
of George III
Oil, on canvas
36¼ × 23½ in. (92.1 × 59.7 cm.)

The right doorway of the Gallery of Italian Art opens into a handsome room of English Jacobean oak paneling which was removed from the Frick summer home, "Eagle Rock", at Pride's Crossing, Massachusetts. Mr. Frick, as may be observed in The Frick Collection in New York, favored an intimate atmosphere rather than the more artificial and formal museum display so much in vogue at the present time. This room as part of his former environment is an important addition to the Collection here. The painting of the woodland scene on the left wall by Théodore Rousseau is reminiscent of Mr. Frick's early interest in the Barbizon school and was one of the first paintings he purchased, in 1896. His delight in portraiture and a preoccupation with the English school is suggested here in the painting of the Princess Sophia, daughter of George III, by John Hoppner on the opposite wall (p. 62). This was one of his latest acquisitions, having been acquired in 1918. On the refectory table below stands a fine Northern Renaissance bronze figure as a candelabra bearer attributed to Peter Vischer the Younger, School of Nuremburg. The rug covering the original oak floor has been described as Persian Bijar design about 1860. A photograph of Mr. Frick rests on the handsomely carved grand piano.

FRENCH EIGHTEENTH CENTURY PERIOD ROOM

VIEW TOWARD NORTHEAST

Opening off the Gallery of Italian Art at the left is a French salon of the eighteenth century. No period could lend itself more auspiciously to a similar setting for it was then that formal conversation was most admired, and a unity of spirit emphasizing the senses and the refinement of taste took precedence. The *boiserie* or wall paneling of French pine with its restrained but decorative carving in this room is from a chateau at Iquebeuf in the Seine-Maritime and dates from the Regency period (1715–1723). The white marble mantel, a little later in date, comes from a nearby chateau at Elboeuf.

Furniture became an important part of the decorative scheme in the eighteenth century. Numerous examples were required for the elaborate building program of the Court which thus determined the taste. Most orders were given for permanent locations in a room, but with the

JEAN-PIERRE LATZ, CA. 1691–1754
Parlor Organ
Marquetry of various woods
Height: 50 in. (127 cm.) open;
29⅝ in. (75.3 cm.) closed
Length: 36⅜ in. (92.3 cm.)
Depth: 22½ in. (57.1 cm.)

development of the salons in Paris small pieces were made to be moved about. Philosophically the utilitarian idea was concealed. One was not only distracted by exquisite ormolu mounts, but elaborate marquetry tended to conceal drawers. Sometimes the tapestry upholstery on chairs matched the wall hangings, and always much attention was given to color. Motifs varied from the elaborate Baroque forms of the seventeenth century, but reduced in scale through Rococo motifs of shells, ribbons and curves, or Chinese figures, to straight lines and the Classical acanthus. Some pieces in their abstract forms must have been thought of almost as works of sculpture. So important was furniture considered that after 1748 a designer to be accredited had to mark each piece. Rue Faubourg Saint-Antoine came to be the center of the industry, but many individuals sold to the crown through the *marchands-merciers* whose originality of design and techniques prevailed during the reign of Louis XVI. Many of the better designers and craftsmen were Germans who had settled in Paris. Their work became so famous that the making of furniture developed into an important industry, continuing even after the Revolution.

Here in this delightful room the furnishings are precious with no awareness of the major or minor arts but attuned to a decorative triumph. One feels it architecturally in the divisions of the

ROGER VANDERCRUSE, 1728–1799
Circular Writing Table
Marquetry of holly wood and
sycamore
Height: 29⅝ in. (75.3 cm.)

MARTIN CARLIN, D. 1785 ▷
Candelabra Table (*Serviteur fidèle*)
Marquetry of tulip wood and
walnut, with Sèvres porcelain plaque
Height: 38 in. (96.5 cm.)

woodwork with its graceful curves, sculpturally in the two Houdon busts, pictorially in the oil
painting above the mantel and the designs inlaid in the furniture and in the pattern of the rug.
This is indeed a tribute to the sensitivity of Miss Frick for the objects were acquired separately.

Of special interest is a small parlor organ (p. 66) believed to have been made for Madame
Adélaïde, the daughter of Louis XV. It carries the mark of Jean-Pierre Latz and also the name of
[François] Duhamel and is in playing condition, and must date about 1750. The elaborate marquetry of floral design has a bagpipe on the top, interestingly enough, similar to the motif in
the paneling above the fireplace which suggests that this room may have been intended as a
music room. Superbly decorated musical instruments were a feature of the eighteenth-century
salon.

Another rare piece is a *serviteur fidèle* or *guéridon* (p. 67), the upper tier of which is fitted with
a Sèvres porcelain plaque and has the mark underneath of Méreaud jeune and the letter x indicating the year 1775. The piece itself has the stamp of Martin Carlin and is typical of his style.
This handsome stand has tulipwood and walnut marquetry and is fitted with ormolu mounts,
the candle holders being adjustable.

There is also a small, round writing table of sycamore and holly wood, the top shelf of which has marquetry of a large floral circle surrounded by a checkered design (p. 67). The cabriole legs have ormolu fittings. It has the stamp of Roger Vandercruse (1728–1799), R.V.L.C., JME, the L and C standing for Lacroix, a French translation of his Flemish name, and the JME standing for *juré maître ébéniste*. All three of the above mentioned men had fine reputations and are known to have worked for the Court, Latz and Carlin having come from Germany. The *secrétaire à abattant* (p. 69) between the two windows is unsigned, but the general style with its straight lines and pictorial marquetry indicates it to be of the late Louis XVI period.

It almost seems as though a heedless and refined society becoming aware of its approaching end wished by quantity to make its mark on posterity. Pierre Verlet, formerly head of the decorative arts section of the Louvre, has identified two side chairs (p. 68) in the room as having been made for Marie-Antoinette for the palace of Saint-Cloud by Georges Jacob (1739–1814), a *menuisier* who may be thought of as creating the final expression of the Louis XVI style. Claude Charles Saunier (1735–1807) who made the console (p. 72) placed against the wall also

JEAN-ANTOINE HOUDON, 1741–1828
Portrait Bust of Madame Houdon
Terra cotta
Height: 19½ in. (49.5 cm.)

JEAN-ANTOINE HOUDON, 1741–1828
Portrait Bust of Claudine Houdon
Plaster
Height: 13¾ in. (34.9 cm.)

lived on into the nineteenth century. Greatly enhancing the room with its warm pink tones is a handsome pile carpet of the type which had become enormously developed at the royal workshops of Savonnerie. This manufactory of long standing had been established by Henry IV in an old soap factory, and hence the name. The room bespeaks the feminine charm of the period.

In the field of portraiture the fantastic skill of the great eighteenth-century French sculptor Jean-Antoine Houdon has hardly been excelled. Beautifully placed on a green marble pedestal in the corner of this room is a charming bust of Madame Houdon (p. 70). Based on some hitherto unpublished correspondence which Miss Frick acquired from the Houdon family she wrote a delightful article about her for the *Art Bulletin,* September, 1947. It tells how during the Reign of Terror there was some question of Houdon's loyalty to the Republic because he had not contributed a patriotic work to the government and because so many of his patrons had been from the aristocracy. Hearing of this Madame Houdon went to Barère of the Committee of Public Safety and explained that her husband was a philosopher and had just done a statue of Philosophy. Houdon had, as a religious commission, just completed a statue of Saint Scholastica

SÈVRES BISCUIT FIGURES,
BY BLONDEAU, 1752, AFTER
FRANÇOIS BOUCHER
La Jeune Suppliant; La Petite
Fille au Tablier
Height: 8¾ in. (22.2 cm.)

◁ CLAUDE-CHARLES SAUNIER,
1735–1807
Console table (console desserte),
teak wood and mahogany inlay,
two-tiered with pierced ormolu
galleries and marble top
Height: 38¾ in. (98.4 cm.)
Width: 38⅛ in. (96.8 cm.)
Depth: 14⁹/₁₆ in. (37 cm.)

holding a book, and Madame Houdon cleverly persuaded Barère that the book was an attribute of Philosophy and that philosophy had prepared the way for the Revolution. It is thought there is only one other authentic version of this portrait of the artist's beautiful wife, a plaster bust in the Louvre.

Of special appeal through the years has been Houdon's busts of children. He seemed to catch their wide-eyed questioning appeal, and nowhere more so than in the small plaster bust of Claudine, his youngest daughter (p. 71). It stands on the console table.

One of the most charming characteristics of eighteenth-century art is its frequent depiction of young children often engaged in adult pursuits. On the mantel are a pair of Sèvres biscuit figures, called Le Jeune Suppliant and La Petite Fille au Tablier, with the incised letters L.T. (p. 73). These were made by Le Tronne who was *sculpteur* at the Sèvres manufactory between 1753 and 1757. The models from which they derive were created in 1752 by the *modeleur* Blondeau, both undoubtedly after designs by François Boucher, although only La Petite Fille au Tablier can be definitely so attributed.

Above the mantel hangs a painting by Jean-Honoré Fragonard (1732–1806) of a boy with a white collar (p.75). One would like to think it a portrait of his son, Alexandre-Evariste, who was born in 1780, and it might very well be, but Wildenstein dates it between 1789 and 1806 which presumably precludes that possibility since the subject appears to be younger than a boy of nine years. Fragonard is known to have done several similar portraits such as the one in The Wallace Collection or one in the Cleveland Museum of Art, and it might be the child of one of his friends. In any case the artist has poeticized the universal appeal of childhood.

Not only does the Museum have another portrait by Fragonard in the large gallery of French paintings, but in the entry to this eighteenth-century room is a small sketch in oil (p.74) which was done as a study for the large panel of *The Pursuit* in the Fragonard Room of The Frick Collection in New York, one of four painted originally for Madame du Barry's chateau at Louveciennes.

GALLERY OF FRENCH
AND FLEMISH ART

VIEW OF SOUTH END OF GALLERY

MASTER OF THE HALF LENGTHS
(HANS VEREYCKE), FLEMISH,
EARLY XVI CENTURY

Madonna and Child with Angel;
Saint Catherine and Saint Barbara
Triptych: oil, on panels
18⅛ × 22⁹/₁₆ in. (46.2 × 57.3 cm.)

This gallery with its beautiful walnut parquet floor, green velvet-covered walls, and sparkling crystal chandeliers contains most of the French paintings in the Museum, and a few in the Flemish tradition. The wonder of Flemish painting lies in the careful observation of nature and the ability to render objects with great accuracy. This became possible because of the discovery of an oil technique in the fifteenth century which was made durable by the use of an enamel-like varnish. It was of course more flexible than the former egg medium. There are three sixteenth-century examples in this gallery done on wood panels which are painted in this revolutionary method. One comes from the region of Douai in France. This region at that time was under the rule of the counts of Flanders. Another came from Lyon, by an artist born in the Hague, and the third from Bruges where the technique originated.

This latter, a triptych (p. 78), represents the Virgin and Child seated in a beautiful realistic landscape. An angel playing the lute appears behind the Virgin, and God looks down from above. The stream and roadway receding into the distance of the woods and the little figures on the bridge are characteristically portrayed. The wings show Saint Catherine in ermine at the left and Saint Barbara reading before her tower at the right. The artist, long identified on stylistic grounds

MASTER OF THE HALF LENGTHS
(HANS VEREYCKE)
Triptych: Madonna and Child
with Angel – Detail:
Angel Playing Lute

JEAN BELLEGAMBE, FRANCO-FLEMISH,
1467/77–1534
Virgin and Child with Rosary;
Saint Bernard and a Cistercian Monk
Diptych: oil, on panels
15⅞ × 20 in. (40.3 × 50.8 cm.)

as the Master of the Half Lengths has now been determined by Otto Benesch to be Hans Vereycke, a follower of Gerard David, who worked first at Bruges and later in Antwerp. Benesch's basis for this attribution was the discovery of a sketch book in which some landscape drawings seemed to have been done directly from nature, lacking, as does the background here, the usual conventions and stylizations of the period. Julius Held feels that Antwerp is the place of origin and that this work must belong to the beginning of Vereycke's career between 1515 and 1520. It is a remarkably fresh example of the essential characteristics of the Flemish school.

A diptych of this Franco-Flemish school is by Jean Bellegambe and forms an important document of the Cistercian Convent of Flines now destroyed (p. 80). Here again the delight of the Flemish artist in the minute rendering of buildings and people in distant landscapes may be seen in the background of the panel representing the Virgin and Child who holds a rosary. The other panel represents Guillaume Bollart, father confessor to the convent, kneeling, and Saint Bernard, founder of the order, standing behind him. This convention of a patron saint seems to have developed in France and here recalls the controversial work of the Master of Moulins, a slightly older contemporary. On the back of this panel one finds a portrait of Jeanne de Boubais, Abbess of

Flines from 1507 to 1533, at devotions (p. 81). She is identified by her coat of arms contained in a millefleurs tapestry. This same heraldic device occurs in the right wing of *The Retable of Le Cellier* by Bellegambe in the Metropolitan Museum of Art, and she is there shown as a kneeling nun before the enthroned Madonna. An outstanding exponent of the Franco-Flemish style, Bellegambe combines the mystical idealism of the Middle Ages with the sensitive observation of physical phenomena characteristic of the Renaissance.

The third example is again a portrait, by Corneille de Lyon (p. 82). He is so-called because, though from the Low Countries, he worked extensively in this French city, making a specialty of portraits, and it is said that Marie de Medici had the wainscoting of a room in the *Hôtel de Soissons* inlaid with some eighty portraits by him. He drew from life directly on the wood panel, thus achieving a vivacity which tends to be lost when the painting is made from a sketch. This example represents, against a characteristic green background, Gabrielle de Rochechouart on the occasion of her third marriage to the Seigneur de Lansac in 1565. It is amusing to note that the small animal of the fur piece worn around her neck has been called a flea catcher. This painting was once in the collection of Jean-Baptiste Colbert, minister under Louis XIV.

If we find in the above-mentioned example a somewhat provincial art burgeoning into international importance we have in the work of Rubens the sophisticated exponent of the grand style of oil painting at its best. He brought the elegance of the Venetian masters to the North and in our portrait we see the Princesse de Condé, Eléonore de Bourbon, in regal attire (p. 83). She had married Philip William of Orange, the son of William the Silent. He had been kidnapped when studying at Louvain and taken to Madrid. Released in 1596 he settled in Brussels. This painting was probably done only a year or two after Rubens' return from Italy in 1608 and at about the time of his appointment as court painter. It is therefore likely to have been entirely the work of his own hand. An inventory of the Marquis de Léganès collection in Madrid of 1655 mentions this painting as being in that collection and "de mano de Rubens". The Princesse died in 1619. This lovely painting, obviously done from life, has all the brilliance of Rubens' work together with his deep understanding of personalities.

The lure of Italy and the Classical tradition was uppermost in the minds of most artists during the seventeenth century, but an earthy interest in realism depicting scenes of humble life had a fascination for centers away from court influences. In 1629 the three Le Nain brothers came from Laon to Paris and achieved a reputation for genre. *Le Bénédicité,* almost certainly by

ANTOINE LE NAIN, FRENCH,
1588–1648
Le Bénédicité
Oil, on copper
5⅝ × 7 in. (14.3 × 17.8 cm.)

Antoine Le Nain, the oldest, is a remarkable example of Northern realism (p. 84). It is done with oil paint on copper and indicates a rare independence for this period. It was formerly in the David Weill collection in Paris.

The eighteenth century is marked by the release of the French national temperament in the service of the arts. Taste radiated from the Court, but more in the sense of creating a fanciful world of gaiety than in the observance of the privileges of aristocracy. It began with the influence of the theatre and the *fêtes champêtres* of Watteau whose spirit dominates the paintings of his fellow townsman, pupil, and ardent admirer, Jean-Baptiste Pater, superbly represented here by *Le Repos dans le Parc* (p. 86). Pater probably accompanied Watteau when he returned to Paris from their home town, Valenciennes, in 1710 or 1711. It was not until the French took seriously the refinements of life derived especially from Venetian influences that Paris became the radiating center of eighteenth-century taste. Pater sensing the consummate skill of Watteau in drawing and in color played a part in this achievement. A pendant to the painting here, called *Les Plaisirs Champêtres,* hangs in the Alte Pinakothek, Munich.

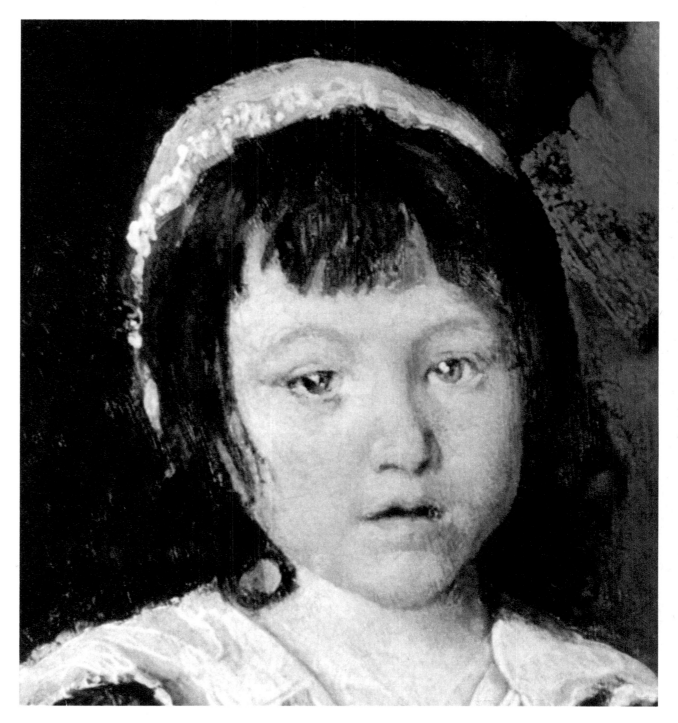

The mood persists in a lovely painting by Nicolas Lancret, entitled *Young Lovers in a Landscape* (p. 87) which hangs adjacent to the romantic painting of the Grotto at Versailles by Hubert Robert (p. 94). This beautiful and well-documented work was included in the celebrated exhibition, France in the Eighteenth Century, held at the Royal Academy of Arts in London in 1968. Lancret was a fellow student of Watteau under Gillot and was greatly influenced by him.

Perhaps no single person was more important in the establishment of French supremacy in the arts during the eighteenth century than Madame de Pompadour. Her brother, the Marquis de Marigny, was given an official position as director general of buildings, gardens, arts and manifestations of the king, a post for which he was well suited, and she herself, besides being a discriminating patron of the arts, encouraged especially the State industries of Sèvres porcelain and Beauvais tapestry. In 1764 when she was not expected to live, Marigny commissioned Carle Van Loo to paint *The Arts in Supplication* (p. 88). It represents the various arts—Painting, Sculpture, Architecture,

JEAN-BAPTISTE PATER, FRENCH,
1695–1736
Le Repos dans le Parc
Oil, on canvas
21 ⅞ × 25 ¼ in. (55.6 × 64.1 cm.)

NICOLAS LANCRET, FRENCH,
1690–1743
Young Lovers in a Landscape
Oil, on canvas
18⅜ × 24⅝ in. (46.6 × 62.5 cm.)

CARLE VAN LOO, FRENCH, 1705–1765 ▷
The Arts in Supplication
Oil, on canvas
30¼ × 26⅛ in. (76.8 × 66.3 cm.)

MAURICE QUENTIN DE LA TOUR, ▷▷
FRENCH, 1704–1788
Portrait of Charles-Marie
de la Condamine
Pastel
19¼ × 17¼ in. (48.9 × 43.8 cm.)

87

JEAN-HONORÉ FRAGONARD,
FRENCH, 1732–1806
Portrait of a Woman Called
Fragonard's Cook
Oil, on canvas
19 × 15¼ in. (48.2 × 38.7 cm.)

NICOLAS BERNARD LÉPICIÉ,
FRENCH, 1735–1784
A Mother Feeding Her Child
Oil, on canvas
17⅜ × 14¼ in. (44.1 × 36.2 cm.)

LOUIS-LÉOPOLD BOILLY,
FRENCH, 1761–1845
La Femme qui Joue de la Guitare
Oil, on canvas
25⅝ × 20⅜ in. (65 × 51.8 cm.)

LOUIS-LÉOPOLD BOILLY
La Femme qui Joue de la Guitare –
Detail: Son of Marie-Antoinette
and Louis XVI

43

HUBERT ROBERT, FRENCH,
1733–1808
Le Bosquet des Bains d'Apollon,
Versailles
Oil, on canvas
24⅞ × 31⅜ in. (63.2 × 79.7 cm.)

and Music—each with his attribute beseeching the Fates not to cut the thread of her life. Above, Destiny remonstrates, while below the grief-stricken crowd protests. When it was exhibited the following year at the Salon de l'Académie Royale de Peinture et de Sculpture, Diderot was enthusiastic. It was mentioned as a missing painting in a catalogue by Louis Réau of missing works by Van Loo published in 1938. When the painting was seen in the gallery here by Professor Jean Seznec it inspired him to do an article on it in the *Gazette des Beaux-Arts* for February, 1974. It seems that Destiny did not listen to the prayers of the Arts, for La Marquise died in April of 1764. This article mentions a letter of distress over her condition from Madame du Deffand to Voltaire. Carle Van Loo died the following year.

It is not surprising that a century which had produced so many distinguished thinkers and had emphasized creative thought, should have been famous for its portrait painters, of whom Maurice Quentin de La Tour was the most outstanding. In keeping with the spirit of the age and perhaps consciously, as indicating the transience of life, he worked in pastel. The portrait of Charles-Marie de la Condamine, thought to have been executed in 1753 after his return from an expedition to

HUBERT ROBERT, FRENCH,
1733–1808
Le Jardin Elysée du Musée des
Monuments Français
Oil, on canvas
24⅞ × 31⅜ in. (63.2 × 79.7 cm.)

the equator to investigate the shape of the earth, shows the internationally famous scientist in a most engaging manner (p. 89).

A characteristic quality of the eighteenth century is the versatility of important painters who often turned to decorative architectural designs, and Fragonard, famous as a decorator, did some outstanding portraits. The not-quite finished portrait of a woman thought to be his cook (p. 90) is an important addition to the gallery. It reveals the bold brush strokes that give vigor to Fragonard's work but which were considered a little too casual for eighteenth-century taste. It is thought to have been executed in 1765 but only recently has attracted attention. It was shown by Wildenstein in Four Centuries of Portraits, in 1945, and again in 1950, in an exhibition of Women in French Painting.

Although one is inclined to think of eighteenth-century art as essentially decorative the tradition of genre and humble life was not overlooked. Because of the emphasis on luxury and the court it was often touched by sentimentality but with the great artists as Chardin or Lépicié, technical refinement triumphs. *A Young Mother Feeding Her Child* by Nicolas Bernard Lépicié is a master-

HUBERT ROBERT, FRENCH,
1733–1808
Adoration of the Magi
Oil, on canvas
14⅛ × 17¼ in. (35.9 × 43.8 cm.)

piece of human sentiment (p. 91). It hangs in its original frame and is signed Lépicié and dated
1774. A study for this is to be found in The Wallace Collection in London.

As a late reflection of eighteenth-century celebrities there is in the gallery, *La Femme qui Joue de
la Guitare* by Louis-Léopold Boilly (p. 92). This represents the Duchesse Yolande Polastron de
Polignac who was the governess of the King's children and a close friend of Marie-Antoinette. The
little boy is her first child. This was exhibited at the last Exposition de la Jeunesse in 1788. Attention
is called to the meticulouly painted, tapestry-upholstered chair so characteristic of the period.

Certainly one of the most active painters at the time of the French Revolution was Hubert
Robert, sometimes called Robert of the Ruins, as interest in our classical past was just beginning to
popularize the beauty of a fallen column or architrave. An example of this is his *Adoration of the
Magi*, painted before 1785 (p. 96). Here, of course, the manger as a classical building in ruin suggests
the Old Dispensation which must now give way to the New. As such this is not a new idea, but
throughout Robert's work one is conscious of the stimulus which his feeling for the past has given

JEAN-LOUIS DEMARNE, FRENCH, ▷
1744–1829
The Seine at Saint Cloud
Oil, on canvas
21¼ × 17½ in. (54 × 44.4 cm.)

97

PERIOD OF LOUIS XVI
Carved and gilt armchair *(bergère)*,
with Beauvais tapestry
Height: 36 in. (91.4 cm.)
Width: 25½ in. (64.7 cm.)
Depth: 23 in. (58.4 cm.)

to his imagination. Even in his representation of contemporary scenes he has chosen subjects of more than a passing interest.

Especially important are his paintings of the gardens at Versailles, for he was commissioned in 1778 when the romantic taste was just forming, to replace a section of the formal gardens with a grotto setting. *Le Bosquet des Bains d'Apollon, Versailles* (p. 94), represents the execution of his idea which was completed in 1781 but no longer exists. An artificial cave was made to represent the palace of Thetis where we see Apollo surrounded by nymphs, a sculptural group by François Girardon, and Thomas Regnaudin, and on either side the Tritons with the horses of Apollo. These latter were executed by the brothers Gaspard and Balthasar Marsy, and Gilles Guérin. The whole forms a charming blend of the classical and romantic spirits. Although Robert never visited Russia, this and another painting of the same size, *Le Jardin Elysée du Musée des Monuments Français* (p. 95), formerly hung in the Pavlovsk Palace. Catherine II and indeed the Russian court was infatuated by the sophistication and refinement of French taste during the eighteenth century and actually made Robert a member of their Academy of Fine Arts. This subject also no longer exists but represents the scene as Robert saw it in 1804, somewhat embellished by trees suggesting the influence on him of his younger days in Italy. The exquisite Diana from the *Château d'Anet* has now been placed in the Louvre, but the column supporting the statue of Abundance still remains

PERIOD OF LOUIS XVI

Pair of carved and gilt armchairs
(fauteuils), with Beauvais tapestry
Height: 39⅜ in. (100 cm.)
Width: 26½ in. (67.3 cm.)
Depth: 23 in. (58.4 cm.)

in situ, now forming the court entrance to the *Ecole des Beaux-Arts.* Other monuments portrayed here, of famous men of France such as Descartes, Molière, La Fontaine, and Turenne, have been removed to the cemeteries of Père-Lachaise or Saint-Germain-des-Prés. As the first keeper of the Louvre after the Revolution, Robert did further service in preserving the art of the past.

Slightly reminiscent of the romanticism of Hubert Robert is the painting, *The Seine at Saint-Cloud,* by Jean-Louis Demarne (p. 97). The palace of Saint-Cloud seen in the upper left background, which was built in 1572, was destroyed by fire during the siege of Paris in 1870. The interest, however, at the time when this picture was painted, early in the nineteenth century, was in the picturesqueness of the scene enhanced by the quaintness of peasant activities. Demarne, whose signature appears in the lower right corner, was born in Brussels. He was interested first in the painting of historical subjects and later devoted his attention to genre and animal life.

The gallery contains some important furniture which gives added interest. A Louis XVI armchair *(bergère)* in Beauvais tapestry (p. 98) is similar to one in the boudoir of Marie-Antoinette at Fontainebleau. There is also a handsome pair of carved gilt armchairs *(fauteuils)* of the same period in which the tapestry upholstery is probably from designs by Boucher as part of a series suggesting the arts and sciences (p. 99). The seats are decorated pictorially with cows, goats, and sheep, thus suggesting the return-to-nature movement prevailing at the end of the century and

PERIOD OF LOUIS XV
Chest of drawers *(bombé commode),*
marquetry of kingwood and
ormolu mounts
Height: 35¼ in. (89.5 cm.)
Length: 51¾ in. (131.4 cm.)
Depth : 23¼ in. (59 cm.)

made familiar by the *hameau* of Marie-Antoinette at Versailles. Scenes on the backs show a young couple studying a globe and an artist at his easel with a young girl looking on. But especially to be noticed is a chest of drawers *(commode bombé)* (p. 100). The mounts are handsome and the basket-weave marquetry of kingwood takes full advantage of the fine woods which became so popular in the mid-century. A console table *(console desserte)* with fluted columns is slightly later (p. 101). It has a marble top enclosed with a pierced ormolu gallery. A beautifully designed ormolu frieze of a guilloche pattern conceals a secret drawer.

Standing on a cabinet (p. 102) in the style of the French Renaissance, at the end of the gallery, is a very fine bronze bust (p. 103), said by von Bode to be of Marcantonio Passeri, a mid-sixteenth century Fleming who lived in Venice, and ascribed by him to Riccio. It seems more likely, however, because of stylistic comparisons to be related to the work of Danese Cattaneo, a seventeenth-century Venetian artist. In any event it is a splendid example of Italian portraiture and once again shows the priority of Italy, not only in bronze casting from the period of the Renaissance but also in portraiture which, as we have seen, was superbly developed in eighteenth-century France.

FRENCH LATE XVIII CENTURY

Console table *(console desserte)*,
mahogany, with Carrara
marble top and pierced
ormolu gallery
Height: 36¼ in. (92.1 cm.)
Length: 48 in. (122 cm.)
Depth: 17½ in. (44.5 cm.)

ITALIAN, VENETIAN, MID–XVI CENTURY
Bronze Portrait of
Marcantonio Passeri, A Fleming
Height: 16 in. (40.6 cm.)

◁ FRENCH RENAISSANCE, CA. 1580
Carved walnut cabinet
Height: 58½ in. (148.6 cm.)
Width: 52½ in. (133.3 cm.)
Depth: 22½ in. (57.1 cm.)

GALLERY OF DECORATIVE ARTS

JEAN-FRANÇOIS DE TROY, FRENCH,
1679–1752
Portrait of a Gentleman
Oil, on canvas
28½ × 23⅜ in. (72.4 × 59.4 cm.)

The Gallery of Decorative Arts is made up of two connecting rooms opening off the larger Gallery of French and Flemish Art. While there is no special emphasis of nationality or style here, several works of great interest are exhibited. There are, in addition to decorative arts, a few paintings and English mezzotints. Among these, in the room at the left, one finds a splendid portrait by Jean-François De Troy (p. 105) in elaborate attire very similar to that seen in De Troy's portrait of the Marquis de Marigny now at Versailles. Although the sitter cannot be identified Monsieur Jacques Vilain of the Ministry of Culture in Paris, who has been compiling a *catalogue raisonné* on the artist, has referred to the painting as a fine example of De Troy's late work, probably done about 1750.

Characteristic of this period, when portraiture in England was reaching its height, are the mezzotints in this gallery of portraits after Reynolds, Raeburn, and Gainsborough. This medium,

FRANÇOIS BOUCHER
Pastorale: A Peasant Boy Fishing –
Detail: Landscape

◁ FRANÇOIS BOUCHER, FRENCH,
1703–1770
Pastorale: A Peasant Boy Fishing
Oil, on canvas
95 × 67 in. (241.2 × 170.2 cm.)

only discovered in the late seventeenth century, became an ideal way to reproduce English portraits where value relationships, with their rich velvety areas, were more impressive than linear characteristics.

But the great achievement of the English artist at this time was in the so-called conversation piece, where a group of people are represented out-of-doors, usually a family on the grounds of their estate, suggesting some activity. *The Gardnor Family* by Arthur Devis (1711–1787) is a typical example of this tradition (p. 109). Three figures are grouped about a small round table in front of an enormous grand piano in a small cleared area. On a hill in the background one sees an elegant domed pavilion. It is amusing how at this time the English gentry wished to show off their property and way of life.

The outstanding object in this room is a red lacquer secretary (p. 110) which was used as a writing desk by Mr. Frick. The upper section has two doors of beveled mirrors, but the numerous drawers and small cupboard within are richly decorated. It is mounted on globular feet and is undoubtedly English, probably from the period of George I when decorating in the Chinese taste was becoming popular. The elaborate carved and pierced ornament at the top is in the manner of Benjamin Goodison, outstanding English cabinet maker. The influence of Chippendale's *The Director* is seen in a wall mirror and nearby ribband-back chair (p. 111).

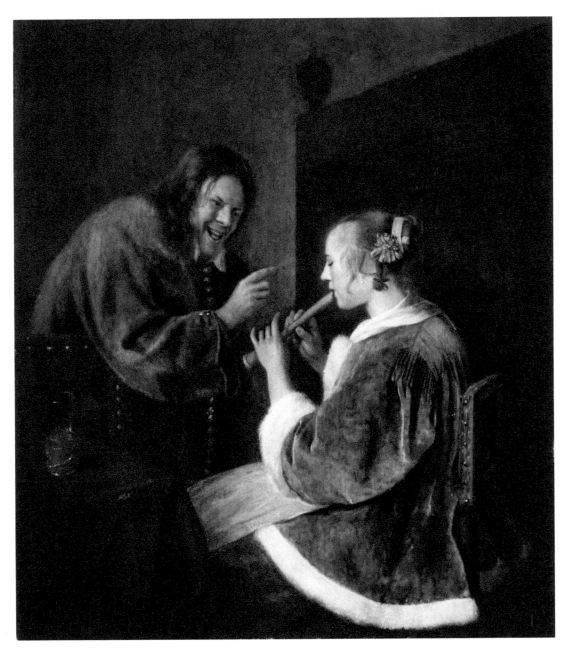

JAN STEEN, DUTCH, 1626–1679
The Music Lesson
Oil, on canvas
12¼ × 10⅛ in. (31.1 × 25.7 cm.)

Passing by an eighteenth-century tapestry screen one enters the other smaller gallery where, immediately on the right, hangs a small Dutch painting by Jan Steen entitled *The Music Lesson* (p. 108). Steen is outstanding among a group of so-called little masters who were active as painters in seventeenth-century Holland. He has been called a humorist, satirist, and moralist; and his paintings always portray a deep-seated understanding of human nature, a cycle of family life. In the Museum example it is said that he himself is the music teacher, his wife, the student intent on the recorder. It is signed Steen in the upper right corner.

Another painting, a large mural-like canvas decorates the opposite wall (p. 106). It is an undated but signed work by François Boucher and listed in Pierre de Nolhac's catalogue of the artist's works published in 1907. Entitled *Pastorale: A Peasant Boy Fishing* this painting is one of a pair; the pendant, *Vegetable Vendor,* is in the Chrysler Museum in Norfolk, Virginia. Here Boucher is the decorator, and one understands his popularity in creating tapestry cartoons for the Beauvais and Gobelins manufactories. The color is fresh and indicates an early work before his palette, influenced by tapestry commissions, became a bit subdued. As a favorite painter of Madame de Pompadour, and her instructor in drawing, he achieved great fame. Although well known because of his exquisite flesh tones and skillful draftsmanship he was innocent of any moral ten-

dencies as recommended by Diderot, or, at the same time, of eroticism. It was enough for him to be a Parisian enjoying life and emphasizing its charm. In this painting in the Museum here one sees how Nature with her beautiful landscapes fits into man's moods. In 1731 he returned to France from four years of study in Italy. He thus had the technical background to play an important role in the development of that great tradition of the eighteenth century when France became the focal point of aesthetic expression.

However, most of this room is given over to handsome vitrines displaying small Renaissance bronzes and Russian silver. One pair of these cases is of black ebonized wood and with gold fluting and the glass held in brass mounts. They are French about 1840.

Small bronzes have long had a special appeal for collectors. We know that the ancient Romans cared for them, and in the middle fifteenth century they became popular in Florence. The lost wax process had been revived and small statuary, inkwells, bells, lamps, and candlesticks were made in large quantities. The transfer of patronage from the Church to the individual at this time meant that bronze became a medium for greater creativity. Their attraction is that by being handled they gain in finish or patina. Florentine, and Paduan artists such as Riccio, dominate the early period but, later, attention shifted to Venice where Sansovino, Danese Cattaneo, and

CHINESE CHIPPENDALE STYLE,
LATE XVIII CENTURY
Carved mirror
Height: 76 in. (183 cm.)
Width: 36 in. (91.4 cm.)

CHIPPENDALE STYLE,
MID–XVIII CENTURY
Carved mahogany ribband-back
armchair
Height: 38¼ in. (97.1 cm.)
Width: 24 in. (61 cm.)
Depth: 18½ in. (47 cm.)

Tiziano Aspetti worked. Influences, of course, quickly spread to Germany and Flanders, and specific attribution is sometimes very uncertain. Wilhelm von Bode's catalogue of the Morgan collection, published in 1910, contains these works which Mr. Frick purchased from Mr. Morgan, but scholarship has greatly developed since then, and many of his attributions seem now questionable. Anthony Radcliffe of the Victoria and Albert Museum in London has made several suggestions in this connection. In 1973, David Owsley, curator of decorative arts at the Carnegie Institute, in Pittsburgh, lectured here at the Museum on small Renaissance bronzes with special reference to the Collection.

Most of the smaller bronzes in the Museum are to be found in the cases in this gallery. One of them, the man standing on a sea monster represents Neptune and was probably executed in Padua early in the sixteenth century (p. 112). Several variations of this, probably a cover for an ink well, are attributed to Severo da Ravenna at one time identified with the Master of the Dragon.

An outstanding bronze in the Collection of very fine quality is a bust of the great Athenian dramatist, Aristophanes, attributed to an artist working in the style of the School of Nuremberg in the first half of the sixteenth century (p. 113). The bronze rests on a wood base of the same period carved with cornucopias and floral motifs and reflecting an Italian influence. Aristophanes

holds with his right hand an open book inscribed with the phrase *Ars Longa* and, with his left, an hour glass and a scroll reading *Vita Brevis*. The saying "Art is long, life is short", so frequently quoted, has been attributed to the Greek physician Hippocrates, active about 400 B.C.

The figure of an old man on a goat (p. 114) is by Pietro Tacca (1577–1640) who worked in Florence and did the grotesque figures of the fountains in the piazza of SS. Annunziata. He was noted for his modeling of animals and was a pupil of Giovanni da Bologna.

The man on horseback (p. 115), is a portrait of Alberico Suardi from Milan, but the artist is unidentified. Its early date from the middle or second half of the fifteenth century as well as its quality gives it a special importance. The achievement of large equestrian statues in bronze marks a high point in the art of that time. This work, however, is not a reduction from a larger work but indicates the beginning of a taste for small bronzes in the home.

Another bronze of considerable importance in the Collection is a portrait of Pope Innocent X (p. 116), identified by von Bode as possibly by Alessandro Algardi who died in Rome in 1654. He was born in Bologna in 1602 and did a larger bust of the Pope, the model of which must have served as the inspiration for this. A similar work in the Victoria and Albert Museum has now been attributed to Domenico Guidi (1625–1701). The likeness recalls the stern and ruthless features of this Pope made famous by Velasquez in his outstanding portrait which is still in Rome. Certainly the work has a classical restraint characteristic of Algardi and the polished border to the cape with the fleur-de-lys motif adds richness and a decorative interest. Baroque tendencies begin to be evident.

Unusual in American museums but most appropriate for one showing the arts of the eighteenth century is a group of eleven exquisite examples of parcel-gilt Russian silver. Their interest lies largely in the shapes and motifs which characterize the Russian heritage where we find a blend of Eastern and Western influences. There had developed in Moscow, the old cultural center, a skill in the metal crafts used largely for religious purposes. Later in the eighteenth century secular and French influences became pronounced. A guild of foreign masters was organized in 1714.

Most of the examples in the Museum were made in Moscow and came from the collection of Jean Herbette, French ambassador to the Soviet Union in the 1930's. Three are illustrated here (p. 117). One, at the left, is a large parcel-gilt beaker or *stopa* on three ball feet with fine repoussé

RUSSIAN, XVII–XVIII CENTURY
Parcel-gilt Silver Vessels:
beaker, *bratina,* covered beaker
Height: 5⅞ in. (14.9 cm.); 5¼ in.
(13.3 cm.); 8¾ in. (22.2 cm.)

embellishment of flowers and leaves. It was made in Moscow in 1737, in the reign of the Tsarina Anna, by a recorded but unidentified silversmith who was active between 1719 and 1750. In the center is one of the most characteristically Russian vessels and an unusually outstanding piece. It is a parcel-gilt *bratina* engraved at the lip with an inscription in old Slavonic characters which translated reads: "Bratina of a good man, Maxim Gregorievich Karamishieva, drink from it to your good health". This is from the period of Tsar Alexei Michailovich, 1660–1680, and was also made in Moscow. The *bratina,* deriving from the Russian word for brother, was used for drinking and toasting—a loving cup—as it was passed around the table. It was also commonly used in the monasteries for the drinking of *kvas* or mead by the monks. The vessel at the right is a tapering parcel-gilt silver beaker or *stopa* with repoussé enrichment of scrolls. The finial on the cover is the Russian Imperial eagle. The name of the maker, Gregory Ivanov Serebrianikov, active 1745 to 1768, is known as well as that of the assayer, Feodor Petrov, active from 1759 to 1774. This work was fashioned in the period of the Tsarina Elizabeth in Moscow in 1760. All of the pieces have the mark of the maker on the bottom. It is only in recent years that significant information about these talented Russian craftsmen working in gold and silver has become available to western scholars. In 1974, Marvin Ross, outstanding authority on Russian decorative arts, gave a lecture at the Museum on Russian seventeenth- and eighteenth-century silver, emphasizing especially these several distinctive pieces in the Collection.

SOUTH CORRIDOR

VIEW TOWARD SOUTH

More noticeable on leaving the building than on entering are the objects in the niches on either side of the bronze and glass entrance gates. At the left is a fine bronze of Meleager and the Calydonian boar after the antique, but probably a Florentine work of the late sixteenth century (p. 120). It, of course, refers to the legend in which Meleager, with the help of his dog, kills a boar, which had been harassing the countryside. The fine modeling bespeaks not only a skillful artist but a full understanding of Renaissance idealism. Classical archaeology had now become very popular, and even in the fifteenth century several ancient bronzes had been excavated which established a fad among connoisseurs.

In the other niche is a small plaster by Jean-Antoine Houdon of a Vestal Virgin (p. 121). Although a student piece from his formative days in Rome which Miss Frick acquired directly from the Houdon family, it is extremely accomplished. He had his inspiration for this from a marble statue of Pandora in the Capitoline Museum of Rome. But unlike Pandora with her box filled with the evils of the world, this figure is holding a lamp, and, as a vestal virgin, might be thought of here as tending the sacred fires of a temple of art.

ITALIAN, FLORENTINE,
LATE XVI CENTURY
Bronze Figure of Meleager and
the Calydonian Boar
Height: 16⅝ in. (42.2 cm.)

JEAN-ANTOINE HOUDON, FRENCH,
1741–1828

Plaster Figure of a Vestal Virgin
Height: 25½ in. (64.7 cm.)

INDEX OF ILLUSTRATIONS

123